T0085879

Caitlin Press Inc.
3375 Ponderosa Way
Qualicum Beach, BC V9K 2J8
www.caitlin-press.com

Text design by Vici Johnstone
Cover design by Andrew Lindesay / Vici Johnstone
Cover image: Still life by Italian painter Giovanna Garzoni (1600–1670). Garzoni was one of the first women artists to paint still life. Image courtesy The Getty Museum Collection.

Printed in Canada

Caitlin Press Inc. acknowledges financial support from the Government of Canada and the Canada Council for the Arts, and the Province of British Columbia through the British Columbia Arts Council and the Book Publisher's Tax Credit.
Library and Archives Canada Cataloguing in Publication

Larder : poems / Rhona McAdam.
McAdam, Rhona, 1957- author.
Canadiana 20210373598 | ISBN 9781773860831 (softcover)
LCC PS8575.A3 L37 2022 | DDC C811/.54—dc23

# LARDER

*Poems*

Rhona McAdam

Caitlin Press 2022

# Contents

# Part 1

"Harmony with land is like harmony with a friend; you cannot cherish his right hand and chop off his left. That is to say, you cannot love game and hate predators... The land is one organism."
—Aldo Leopold

## Anna's Hummingbird

When the hummingbird plummets,
a whistling blur through the plum blossom,
it will be spring. He woos
with his crimson throat, his emerald coat.

It's the apple tree this year.
Gnarled and mossy branches
hold treasure. Two pearls
in a basket of twigs and down
and spider silk, walls spackled
with mud and lichen.

Invisible in her grassy browns she rocks
with her cradle while the wind
strums and plucks the leafless boughs
and the rain sheets its verticals.

In sunlight she glitters, green
gilding her feathers, a ruby
beneath her chin. Fearlessly small,
her language a fizz of clicks
and chitters from the highest branch,
her flight a whirling maternal buzz.

She declares
that summer is imminent
that the nestlings will fledge
together, and part
to hector and battle at the feeders
and there will be scarlet blossom
to feed them all.

# Wild Bees

We, we multitude
sun–blossomed on leaves or
dark–spotting petal
pistil stamen. Knowing each
flower's golden mean.
Sweet comfort there
for our young.
Priming our baskets
with pollen.
A day's work
and a day's work and a day and a day
more. All this purpose
purpose purpose.
The weeds the woods
the garden.
Those single single
destinations, never mix this
with that:
one source in its
many places.
We fly, we crawl, we gather.
And again.
Our futures waiting to be lardered.
So many homes
we have, our
dark places, combed and tunnelled,
crumbed with our comings and goings.
The neatness of our labours:
eggs entombed
with food
for an afterlife
we will not witness.
Our one season this
duty, duty.

## Wasps

One false step and they seethe from a fissure
beneath my feet—a quiet spot
they've chosen. A subterranean colony
growing all summer, workers peeling my walls
and door jambs, descending to build
a palace of paper and spittle.
I stand quite still as they hasten around me.
Not yet undone, though frost is coming.

What is their larder these brown days
as the world turns fickle? The queen's scent
fades. All colour and sweetness are gone.
No wonder there's only hunger raging
now the future has launched itself
to hide in every crack and leaf and crevice.

# Wireworm

Its ancestors slept for months in the bellies
of sailing ships, disembarked in ballast
gifted to our shores;
made their way like pioneers
feeding on the fat of their land.

Just as today it waxes
in the crumbling dark:
a pale, gold sliver of moon
ancient in its segmented suit
its thin translucent bristle like the chin
of a young farmer. Or the brow
of an old one, bending to the ground
to pluck a worm from its bed.

Its medium is soil, its enemies few.
When we drown it, it rises
to new life. Starvation
stills it for a season. Poison
gives it pause
to convalesce in its food beds.

In summer it decamps
into cooler depths,
rises to bask in moisture
that keeps its food supple
and succulent.

Lover of grasses
and grains, it seeks the perfume of starch
and decay. Makes catacombs
in potatoes, mines black shadows
in carrots. Noses a root tip, tastes its way
to the next, and the next. Makes ladders
inside the stems of seedlings,
resting in its tubular meal
until its host withers
and falls.

## Tent Caterpillars

All the long spring
they've been hatching:
black worms, numerous
and immaterial;
spinning tents
in the branches
to house a communal appetite,
falling from their shrouds
in long black drops.
Growing into their skin
and gilding bristle,
until, lions at last,
they bask on tree limbs
in the heat of noon,
emerging from torpor
in the cooling air.

We swear we hear them
whiskering up the walls,
their thousand fingers
caressing our roofs
and chimney pots.
Their soft black patience
lingering on our windows
watching us eat.
Raking their hunger
along leaf-lines,
carving as they feed
the story of their bodies' garden,
swelling with the season,
and one day
leafing like autumn wings.

# Spider Season

Sticky with light, webs block our way
if we see them, and more often
drape our missteps,
something we must battle
as if prey, as if we needed
this reminder of what it is
to be small, and trapped,
and surprised
by the inescapable.

The spiders grow large
this time of year,
their bodies plump
and well written,
the runes inscrutable
until we stop
to watch their delicate needles
turning and turning death
in its long grey envelope
so tenderly composed
at the edge of the jewelled trap.

We saw them back in spring
perhaps this was one
no larger then
than a running speck
amidst a cloud of them
forming and reforming
their gauzy constellations
between the plants.

Today she is poised on the lintel.
She will mate, and collect, later,
the stricken male
to spin him into her larder.
And we will walk again
into her filaments, breaking patterns,
perhaps unhook in passing
ignorance, the fluff
of her golden egg.

## Evolution of the Tick

They wear
their sex on their backs, their
waistbands are
infinite.
Their DNA
wraps them round grasses
leaving four arms free
for the ride.
They slide
between leaves in our books
stopping to blacken
a favourite word.
They are
messengers of heat
and heartbeat.
They slip
eight legs and a metaphor
under our doors, pause
in postures of creep
on night's walls.
On us
they crawl indiscernibly skywards,
males tangling in the long grass
of our thinking caps, seeking
the anchored female
in an ancient quest:
sex and blood, sex
and blood.

## Cordyceps

The ant has been infected
with the need to climb

its mind hollowed of the urge
to tunnel through wood

now it sees only
the vertical bark

all it has left are the stars
and the struggling up

while the fungus rides
the ant's mind with the whips

of instinct. Their needs
are the same, and the ant

climbs, carrying them together
to the top of the tree where

the fungus roots the ant
to the branch, and fruits

sending its stars to the wind.

# Aristotle's Lantern

*In reality the mouth-apparatus of the urchin is continuous from one end to the other, but to outward appearance it is not so, but looks like a horn lantern with the panes of horn left out.*

—Aristotle, *Historia Animalium*

Who named you urchin? No imp
with that devil mouth: pentangle in a spiny orb.

Five teeth and a tongue and
fifteen hundred breathing-arms.

Five hundred million days asleep in stone bedrooms
you scoured from the ocean's flank with unstoppable teeth.

Five hundred million nights roaming the food beds
with your dark lanterns.

Lover of fives, the untouchable number.
Untouchable in your cloud of spines.

In clouds of your fellows you cleave the stems of sea-forests,
kiss stone into sand, bring bridges to their knees.

Your teeth grow into their blades. Nothing
can dull them, gaining edge from injury.

You embrace the dark in your brittle centre.
You are the eye, every cell shrinking from light.

Your barbs bristle towards danger, bury a poisoned cusp
in your enemies. Regrow lost splinters.

You cast your children out into the sea.
They grow into arrows: two arms and a mouth

and five terrible teeth
strong enough to eat you.

## Skate

In dark waters
my inscriptions washed away
I am a great slate, or

blank paper, turned
by the sea's wind.

I flutter like a falling
message from
the blue air above

where the fishermen breathe
a livelihood big enough to turn
those engines.

I am as light
as my liquid world
night's shadow among the plankton

plying my hunger
as I am patterned to do

but the nets, breathing current,
surround the little world
that gathers unwillingly
in their throats.

All of us
prey and hunter, school and solitary
lifted to an air too dry
to breathe, awaiting

official word on whether fish
feel pain, and until then
what to make of this

swift knife
the living descent of the torso
wingless, a piece-meal for something.

On shore
the basket of wings
twitches, like the limbs
of a sleeping dog.

# Table

The table often dreamt it was an animal.

But if it were an animal, it could not be a table.

If it were an animal, it would have run with the others
when the chainsaws came to take the trees
which would become tables.

In the house, a woman comes every night
and passes a warm cloth over its back
as if it were an animal.

On its four legs
the table could run away from the house.
But it thinks of the chairs that surround it: it knows
an animal does not abandon its young.

What the table likes best is when the woman tickles it
while she gathers the breadcrumbs
left by the children.

*From the Spanish: "Mesa" by Juan Carlos Galeano*

## Sara at Sixteen

You walked from my family past
into my present, bringing your mud,
your stink, your hair—my lord
your hair, fastened to the car seats,
pillowed in the vacuum,
autumnal clumps on every rug.

Now you are the star
of my home movie, my silent
back seat driver. No walk
but with you. No meal
but with you beneath the table,
your leftovers to consider,
doggie bags a literal
on every outing without you.

Now that I am yours,
you tell me you are old
and must leave me. You walk
suddenly this year with pain
and stiffness; gradually this year
fall behind me on the path.
You grow confused, and bark
randomly at night, forgetting why.

Yet you frisk like a puppy
with other dogs, though it costs you
later, that glee. And your joy
at an open door, the rattle
of keys, is undiminished
even now you must be lifted
to the back seat of my car.

Yet your gaze could cure
multitudes, the silk of your head
soothe any worry.
You teach us to taste
each morning as if it's our first.

And day after day you lie
near my feet, dreaming and fixed
on some distant thing that is, at last,
outrunning you.

# Dog, Running

In the other room the dog is running in some
precarious place he knows. Forming its name
between gritted teeth, he chews and whiffles its syllables
in the language of that land, which he visits often.

The forays we make in my world
only lure him back to that inner meadow
seeking the twilit pack who wait for him at the water's edge,
their tracks settling in the sand, the meaning of their scent
imponderable, and worthy of long reflection.
Are there people there, or rabbits? I suspect only dogs
who challenge my existence, calling him by some
wild name, drawing him farther into their darkness.

Sometimes I brush him while he sleeps.
The brush mats so quickly with his fur
I think it is dreams seeping from his pores
hair by hair. They travel around the house,
assemble themselves into clouds on the floor
that riffle when we pass.

When sunlight reaches
into these rooms, his dreams glint
on every surface, the house becoming dog
in the shine of its nascent pelt. He lies down in that,
as if this is the path he must follow to leave this place
as if rehearsing for the dream in which
his work here is done.

# Bear Dreams

The bear entered my dream
on two legs. Paced the perimeter
of my home like a Zuni fetish,
burdens of meaning lashed
to his back in packages
of precious stone.

I might have been a fish
he tossed from water,
left for dead,
choking on sleep.

From my bed I can trace
the path he wore: it slides
like a necklace round my life
and between my breasts
hangs the face of all
that restlessness: two eyes,
two ears, and the rest
best left to sleep's pinhole camera.

Sleep is what summoned him
after all, through the winter's slumbering
snow. I dread that careless dream
that invites him back again, a claw
unzipping the fabric of sleep.

# Culatello

*In 1881, Parmesan poet Giuseppe Callegari named Culatello and la bomba di riso
as the foods that would be served in Paradise.*

On the flatlands beside the Po
black pigs graze beneath the slender trees,
growing fatter than the land.

A good life, well-lived
they say, shepherding you
to the end of it,
and into the next.

Shorn of your bones
you are bathed in wine,
massaged with salt
and rested.

When you next appear,
little bottom in your string vest,
it's hanging in cellars
by your hundreds,
meaty pears, pendulous
in a darkened orchard.

Po breezes wrap you in flora,
their bloom between the threads
a soft grey down
to blanket you.

You dwindle
through the summer heat
and winter mists, meditating
on wine and spice, until

for that last meal you are shaved
thin as tissue, stained glass
against the light,
a wafer of flesh melting
upon a grateful tongue, becoming,
in some long tomorrow,
other flesh.

# Part 2

"First we eat, then we do everything else."
—M.F.K. Fisher

# Parma Triptych

## 1. Parma

A town, they say, built on whey. From the cheese, for the pigs. A town that reeks from the fields at blood and bone time, when the wind is in disfavour. Else Aqua de Parma, and the sweet scent of prosperity are all you'll get between mealtimes, clattering the cobbled streets on your bicycle, free hand raising an umbrella when it rains, never using your bell. This town welcomes visitors by air with an airport roundabout whose centre holds a tree trained to be a biplane, and at another an evergreen Verdi plays forever his leafy grand. Somewhere there should be others, wheeled like a cheese, or fattened like a ham. There should be gilded tortelli on the streets and Lambrusco staining the fountains.

## 2. La Croce di Malta

Enter from a courtyard where the crumbling façade of a church keeps the time fixed, let's say, at three-fifteen. The doors are glass, the handles chrome. Inside, Signora never hurries. She takes you always to the same square table, positioned with a view of the doorway, your back to the knick-knacks. The placemats are paper, white with black pots that loop around the edge. The silverware shines, the glasses are large and the menu takes you a year to make sense of; by when you've sampled its finest, the vivid reds and greens of its sauces pooled on the gleaming plates, the modest ecstasy of texture imprinted on memory.

## 3. Vitello Tonnato

A leap, to invite the union of earth and sea on one plate. A puddle of mud if ever there was. Slurry, something unholy hidden beneath. Faith takes the fork and feeds you a mouthful beyond definition. Salt and softness and something like lemon. Flesh that dissolves its memory on the tongue and then lingers, an old friend with many long confessions, a pungent mesh of secrets teased out into half-familiar strands.

# Implements

What more inviting than a kitchen
of dull knives, and no steel to hone them,
no peelers, no scrapers, no whisks, a room
bereft of implements, reason enough
to navigate the narrow streets of this town,
its purveyors coved in cobbled alleyways,
*buona sera signora* between
the crowded shelves, welcoming
with their hands, deft with special instruments
for retrieving stock from above
or window displays or the drawers of treasure
arrayed out of reach and sight.

A knife shop yields up its blades
of rippled steel, its handles of olive and yew,
the long pale teeth of porcelain, too sharp,
bone sharp, fierce enough to shatter on tile.

The shop of the copper pots stays lidded
in mystery, its hours as odd and random
as its wares, from which chance gleams
sometimes emanate through shutters.

From the shop across the river
a *frullatore*, tool for frothing milk; and a bowl
of beaten copper; and a knife
for slicing meat, green-handled,
the instrument of butchers, their fearless hands
in chainmail. The glass seller sells us stemless
*bicchieri*, thin as light, round as a new moon.

At the market, tablecloths fly like flags
from scaffolding, they tent around us
and the *signore* fingering the cloth and gathering
their hues into big white bags
for the homeward journey.

Home, this temporary nest, is fattening
with our swag, drawers straining to close,
the fridge a work of balance,
and something, at last, steaming towards supper
in a stranger's heat-stained pots.

## Croutons

You accuse me of always making croutons
when you call. As if the phone can fill
the house with toasting bread,
essence of garlic, the smoke of oil
crisping the crumb.

And yet, you do not refuse
this little raft of cheese,
hiding in its skirts
a bay of onion. You spoon
its depths, an oarsman
skilled in such heavy terrain.

This copse of lettuce
scattered with rusk
still pleases you;
you welcome home
each morsel of crust
from the casserole.

# Cheese

*A cheese may disappoint. It may be dull, it may be naive, it may be over-sophisti-
cated. Yet it remains cheese, milk's leap toward immortality.*
                                        —Clifton Fadiman

Milk is the miracle we are learning
atom by atom. It is short on vitamins
and full of fat. It has less water
than most vegetables. These things we know,
but its murk and lipids yield secrets
unimaginable, unpronounceable.

We gaze at the words scrolling above us
on the screen, their fractured English only
half recognizable. The hairy beauty
of the casein micelles in their diagrams,
their migration into flocks, freed from their
hydrophobic fractions, transfixes us.

We are diving in beyond the cellular:
far from home, we too are colloidal, carbon
atoms parting from our hydrogen, leaving
a trail of water and broken bonds in our wake,
like the trail of the shepherd, his precious
saddlebag sewn from the stomach of a lamb
filled with the morning's milk, churning as he rides
into the sunset of his great discovery.

# Abbey Root Cellar, February

The kitchen door divides the clatter
and perfume of dinner from a silent
underworld. We follow the sloping floor
to a hive of low ceilings and rooms
cut from summer soil, step soundless
on packed earth as if walking
the monastery's grounds,
pacing out prayer with the brothers.

A trail of light flows from dark to dim
to a pale bulb swinging from its rope.
In the room of potatoes
the frost seeps upwards,
turning their flesh soft and sugary.
There is an urgency to their use.

In the room of carrots we feel them
beneath our hands, breathing through sand,
root hairs seeking moisture and solid earth.

Tall jars on long shelves in all colours.
Preserving is work
and work is prayer, and this is a wall of it.
Each summer the monks make jam
from the orchard fruits, pack
tender bodies in syrup. Pickles. Kraut.
Peas and beets and beans from the gardens.
The year has passed its midpoint;
gaps mar the patterns like lost teeth.

Above us the work carries on.
Vespers in the chapel. Chants losing threads
each year. Time overtaking the garden,
its form a shadow beneath the snow,
custodians moving more slowly than winter.

## Caramelized Garlic & Squash Tart

Blind baking in another strange kitchen
I miss so much what is stashed so far away
in the farthest reaches of my cupboards: those baking beads,
shiny pearls of heavy clay, hauled from England,
snug and greasy in their brittle plastic tub. The pastry,
you see, is not cooperating, its layers of butter and dough
too multiple for the shape I am forcing by gravity
upon it. It has ideas of altitude
I seek to discourage, stabbing it with my fork,
laying makeshift weights upon it, anticipating a sticky
revenge that takes two of us and a small sharp knife
to undo. Fretting, I have already peeled and sectioned the squash,
a golden nugget from last year's harvest, its warts and strips
falling away from the blade of this inadequate knife,
the seeds a knot of treasure I untangle from an orange net
and lay out to dry for next year's garden, while its flesh softens
in the oven in yellow oil that's fretted with thyme.
I free the garlic from its waspy papers,
blanch its sprouting, off-season cloves in water,
bathe them in hot oil till they brown and evolve in the pan,
smothered in vinegar and herbs, sugared and watered,
reduced to a fine black sap that fools the unsuspecting eye—
as if olives or raisins—infusing the hallways with pheromones.
In time, I crack eggs, so fresh their whites are jellyfish
in the bowl, and beat them violently with a fork, adding a drift
of sour cream. I lay the squash and garlic on pastry,
crumble cheese as white and soft as the snow beyond the window,
pour eggs and cream and scatter thyme and pepper
over all. Nothing to do now but wait, while aromas
creep beneath doors and the tart turns golden in the heat,
transforming unruly neighbours into family, celebrating
their differences, conjoining them on the altar of appetite.

# Cutlet

Whatever you were
you have now become other.

There is no way to identify
from this gristle, from this

uncuttable dark shape on the plate
what larger shape you breathed

or how long you walked,
ran, toughened on this earth.

What I face has no name,
no identifying condiment.

Inside this skin of coating
you are grey, your flavour only 'meat.'

How then to court you
on this plate of woe?

Where my knife approaches
you grow skittish, escaping

to the plate's borders, forging a trail
of grease and porridge-crumb

through the starch and vegetation
until you are alone. Unyielding.

No softening of your position
on the fork. And so I grant you

emancipation, a return
to the earth that fed you,

that one of us at least
may leave this meal redeemed.

# Meat

For all we have eaten we are
no more than we were. Their souls
escaped when they left those
useful bodies, made fat for us.

Habits of menu undo them;
less our hunger than our taste
for grazing, roaming as we do
the pastures of plenty,
hunting with our plastic trays,
easing open the Styrofoam
for our young.

They will find platters and tins
to house them at the ends of their lives,
as unremembered as they were
unnamed. They were
landscape to us, happy
in the fields or warm and fragrant
in their barns, lowing
over baby Jesus.

We never see them
in the lifelong dark
of their little, brutal worlds
or pastured in shit, chewing
the cud of pill and pellet.

Their herdsmen are steel and smoke,
they will die at no man's hand.

# Dry Ribs

If we were in the desert
we could make of these
a landscape:
dunes of mashed potato,
boulders of gristle and bone
the colour of volcanic rock,
of spoor, of buffalo hide.

Our desert would be
a salty place. Here we could
parch to death:
seasoned warriors, too tough
to die, blasted by heat,
haloed by vultures.

Our desert would shine
like oil, beneath
the scorched sand that smothers
sinew and bone. But
white the dunes, white
to the horizon. This desert
is no place for green.
Plants would only die here
a long soft death.

Forge then, your painful way
across our desert. Where dunes
eventually end, the bones
lay their enduring trail, untouchable,
no succour for lost travellers,
a memory we'll leave in our wake:
a cairn of suffering; blackened stars
in a moonless sky.

# Gravy

Who'd want to live
in a world without gravy,
which makes all things
equal on the plate,
which gives potatoes
a smooth ride, which
comforts the meat
it came from.

If gravy were the world
there'd be no war,
just happy islands
in a savoury sea; we'd all
be warm enough in our blanket
of brown. There'd be no need
for knives; we could curl forever
in the wombs of ladles.

Floured or cornstarched,
thickened or reduced,
let it line your plate
like the fabric of childhood,
and sign its name
on the Sunday roast,
let it swoon in your Yorkshires
and kiss each vegetable goodnight.

## Fish Sticks

Faux fish, a battered shred
of what once swam, ate, breathed
its last in a smother of kin
somewhere mid-Atlantic, or flew
choking from a fish-farmer's net.

Reduced to what now: hard shreds
of body in a coffin of grease.
A line of white between
two of dull wheat,
their sullen leather rubbing wrong
the knife.

Robbed of shape,
texture, taste, what are you:
aroma of tideline, midden,
whale breath.

No loaves, no fishes
from the scrapings
off these plates.

Trawlers still mine
your ancestral run, hauling
random species to their decks,
sowing the dead
into waters that close, stone
silent, on their wake.

## Lake Lenore Whitefish

They are arranged
headlessly under tinfoil,
ready for serving, no implement
provided but our own
ingenuity. Table knives part the flesh
but not the skin. Forks part the skin
but cannot grip what remains:
we lift our share and it scatters
wet flakes on the baking sheet.

The tails a row of smirks,
picket fence, end of line.

And when we hunters we
gatherers make our way
plunderous to the table
the real work begins.
We are each
a fisher of bones.
Some find them by mouth,
whiskering between bites;
others choose knifework,
making lace on the plate,
a hayrick in the bone bowl,

until we are all replete, wondering
at the whiteness of it:
the fish, the potato,
the weary plate, the snow
falling outside the window and beyond,
falling tonight on Lake Lenore.

# Salad

Such atrocities in your name:
sculptures of jelly and cabbage;
ring moulds, milky and pink;
canned fruit and marshmallows.

When all that was asked
was leaf from the garden, something green
and difficult to fork, torn in pieces
too large to eat daintily. Hazardous food    .
in its dressing, indelible oils on clothing,
vinegar to catch in the throat, fragments
to catch on teeth and green the smile.

In a London supermarket, the greening face
of the check-out boy who dropped
the cellophane Little Gem at the sight
of the trapped wasp within,
yet what comfort to find a life enduring
the sprays, the harvest, the washes,
all those backs and hands and machines
that cleaned its connection to dirt
and placed it with its many twins
in the bin marked lettuce:

a bin among many, all heaped impossibly high
to comfort us, that we not face bare shelves
or imperfection, living as best we can
our reality in front of the TV.

But warm duck gizzard
on young lettuce in a Paris café
when the world unfolded its napkin
in your lap. When radishes were pink
and crisp in the salt you dipped
them in on picnics. When grated beets
and celeriac never failed to cheer
on a dull day in a strange language.

## Roasting Vegetables

Into a clean and quiet mouth
of heat they go, the carrots
cubed and singing in their coats
of oil, buttoned with salt, the onions
fringed with black, all sugaring as they curl. Garlic
there is, plump crescents ripening
into harvest gold with the squash,
the potatoes, and the soft bellies of zucchini
revealing their nascent seeds
as they slump.

We'd like to believe
they rolled in from the garden,
processions of plenty,
innocent and clean, shrugging off
their origins in dirt, black residue of growing things
that passed with care through this kitchen,
and returned to the soil.

But these are travellers
from distant fields, the yield
of unknown labours, paragons of shape
and size to suit the aims of commerce,
protected as they grew
from tooth and nail and wing
by any means expedient
and so beneath their skins
the signatures of science and economy
engrave themselves in characters too small
for us to see; our bodies to read
and reveal to our older selves
or our children's children the product
of the sum of the parts we have been
holding on our tongues in trust
these many years.

# Bananas

Who'd have thought to do that
to a banana, she asks of the golden discs
fringed with sugar that tile this loaf
so carefully, containing odd blacknesses
where the heart of a banana bled into batter,
its sweetness colouring as it baked.

Full of surprises, these tubes in their sunshine wrappers:
nature showing us how to package. Unzip one
and it never fails to follow its line, dropping hems
in its haste to emerge, these lobes
so bland and pleasureful.

Pull another trick from the hand
of bananadom: lay them
peeled naked, sliced long and resting
on their cuts, on a baking dish
bedded with thin sheets of butter.
Strew them with brown sugar and bake
till the scent torments you from the table.
Pillow them, hot, in dishes of ice cream
the colour they once were. They will melt
like the softest heart.

# Fruit Cake

Raisins, greying,
and the buckshot of currants
have lost the desire for round.

Apricots cubed into sticky gold
with fraying pineapple
and lumps of peel.

Cherries, gone glassy with sugar,
forget they were ever fruit,

all drenched in brandy and left
to remember the shapes
their skins abandoned
all those summer days ago,
drinking the liquor until the bowl
exudes lost grapes.

Nuts cracked at a kitchen table
until fingers ache, then chopped
with an old blade in an old handle.

This is your foundation,
the rest a mortice,
a labour of eggs and flour and fat,
its heaviness a wish
upon a wooden spoon, child's hand
beneath a mother's,
turning a hard tide once,
twice, thrice, invoking luck,

luck with the buried coin,
the bounty of fruit, of hands
on the spoon,

until the pebbled mass
folds into the tin to rest in a long heat,
stained glass for the season ahead.

# Jello

O red mystery, o berry
of childhood's branch.

Powder of my school lunchbox,
a fingerdip surprise
for snack time, cherry dust
in a Tupperware nest.

O red iceberg, wobbling
on the tray, perfect
in your thick white bowl,
ridged like a glacial erratic,
mirroring the spoon's imperfections.

Each spoonful must be pulled
by suction past the lips
to melt and sweeten
on the tongue.

O magical food,
too red to be real.

# Coffee

It was coffee in the kitchens of then.
Aluminum pot on the stove,
electric for special occasions.

The burping that underwrote mealtimes,
grit at the bottom of the cup, a morsel
to chew on while waiting for pie.

A rite of passage, that bitter sip
to fill the cup in truck stops
its surface feathered with white
while the cream travelled down,
mushrooming from the depths.

Breakfasting in coffee shops
the dull lip of cup, white
with a green line, a snug fit
to its saucer, the square of napkin
soaking the drips between.

Coffee came in cans then,
with hard black candies
pictured on the packaging. That gasp
when the opener bit the edge.
Black crumbs that bore
no relation to anything living
clung with winter passion
to the sides of spoons, counter, pot.

Something elemental, we supposed,
like sugar or flour, mined
from some foreign hill.

## By the Glass

Free for the taking
through all my childhood,
crashing into glasses bouldered with ice,
poured thickly from the sides of plastic jugs,
the unremarked and neglected
sentry at the top of place settings,
sweating on Formica,
seized to cure fits of coughing
or moments of spice, replenished
unasked and endlessly.

When the costly bottles came,
in thalassic greens and fluvial blues,
the taps still turned for the frugal,
and we got what we paid for,
tepid, swirling with mist, fragrant
with swamp, or sold for 10p a glass
at a parsimonious caff in Cornwall.
We drank each chlorinated drop
and spared the tip.

In New Mexico restaurants,
cards propped on the tables
invited us to value even this, the stuff
of dishpans and swimming pools,
while all afternoon in the Hilton
the self-flushing toilets
thundered their copious refrain
in unoccupied stalls.

A friend has returned from Africa.
We sit on the beach in clothes the colour of sand,
watching clouds gather
on the undrinkable blue horizon.

# Part 3

"Shall I not have intelligence with the earth?
Am I not partly leaves and vegetable mould myself?"
—Henry David Thoreau, *Walden*

# Hügelkultur

In the body of the tree, other lives
grow dank and vibrant.

This is the road, this is the table,
this is the world
that feeds a smaller world
and worlds within.

The tree unlearns its age,
rings dwindling as it falls back
into germinating earth.

See how its roots make a river
of appetite, its branches
a temporary bed. Water runs through them
and air. The whole a breathing mass
inhaling the sun's work, exhaling the moon.

No moments of stillness in transformation.
The process of becoming
summons a cast of trillions.
*Bacillus subtilis. Pseudomonas fluorescens.*
Teeth and mandibles, slime and excreta.

Over and under the rats the nematodes
the micro-armadillos. Flow of life on death.
Mycorrhizal fungi fingering their way,
the micro micro organisms
detritivores not yet counted or named.

Down, down in the belly
of the earth, there is life
hungry for its dinner,
living out its destiny in the vast
unequal world of dark and damp decay.

## Tasting Dirt

Earth called me to its table
and I became its fork, its knife, its
roundest spoon. My teeth
were its pebbles, my tongue
wormed the blackest
reaches, seeking to unite
its minerals, its dank organic matter,
its shit and water, and the white wires
of roots, which thirsted
in curtains for the deep,
and never reached it.

I ate the dirt that welcomed me;
that sang beneath my shovel
its guttural songs, its parables
of wind and weather; that turned
its belly to the sun, its back
on winter; that swallowed
our seed, our water, our blood
and unfolded its hand of marvels.

Beneath the moons of my nails
it laid down its black horizons,
imprinted its reckonings
in each line on my hands. Bruised
my face and gritted my hair.
Ran off my body
and back to ground
each night. Carried me with it,
dead leaves of my skin,
broken stalks of my hair,
making up the ancestral bed.

## Early Apples

Now summer has ripened
to its midpoint, the apples
are in suicide, green bodies
on the lawn each morning, perfect
but for that one round bruise
or the rusting holes,
perhaps the work of birds
who have already stripped the plum
and cherry trees, flung
half-eaten fruit to the ground,
winged vandals chittering
in lofty crowds.

I have climbed
into the apple tree with my bucket,
the very ice cream pail
my mother used for berries.
I have filled my fridge
with round green fruit
and called the neighbours. Tomorrow
I will pare and freeze the flesh.
I will run the juicer till my feet ache
from standing, I will fill the compost
with brown sweet trimmings. There will be
apple cake and pastry, apple sauce
and apple butter. Apple with the berries
blackening among the thorns. My poor
scratched arms aflame with summer.

# September

These diminishing mornings
honeybees find pleasure in blue,
spiky clouds of sea holly
or gassy flames of borage
dropping slivers of sky to the ground
with each last visit.

This late and still the bees
return to the hives laden,
setting store for the winter, brood
slowing as the queen marks the angle
of sun, the patterns of rain,
the shifting colours of pollen.

The end of flowers, too:
roses pushing their fruit where blossom
once fed so handsomely; apples swollen
and round, their perfect circumference
set in spring, the orchard bees
gone now, their legacy seeded
in tubes and tunnels.

Blackberry blooms on a cooling thread
of summer light. This last
white bounty fills the comb, how it drips
when the racks are lifted, the nectar
not yet set or sealed. But soon
the nectar will be gone, and with it
the summer, the sun's liquid slowing
to an autumn haze.

## Wild

The smallest, said the fruit seller,
are always the sweetest.

And seeking this
I have flayed my arms
in the woods all week
following the hooked green path
of vine, the violet crumbs
of the trailing blackberry.

Sparse and elusive, it takes an eye
to find them, an age to fill
the picking bowl.

They must be rolled and gentled
from the branch: one wrong move
and they bruise, weep
their thin red honey.

Sorting them
from their crowns of fluff, their
grass seed wreaths
is work for elves. Microscopic. Maddening.

Their flavour is catastrophic;
the palate
experiences rebirth;
lust sends appetite
into the woods to pray.

# Woods

A new trail with its own unique warnings
Here, uneven pavement
is the named hazard. No mention of joggers
swinging too close on the path
then slapping on to the lookout.

Otherwise just rain for company
meagre through the canopy.

Arbutus trees
list curiously. On closer inspection
their slender trunks not only curve
but make right angles.
Some urgent yearning
for sunlight long ago
has been layered into permanence.

Seemingly not the right decision
for they twist still in the understory.

One has folded itself in the crook
of a Douglas fir that leans
away from responsibility,
preoccupied by gravity.
When it's had enough it will
simply fall: roots, splayed and shallow,
go vertical.

One day, washed clean,
those roots will show their hand,
a message of chronic thirst
and ornamental crowding, to whoever
braves the heaving pavement.

# Garry Oak

My lawn's anchor, fissured trunk ribbed
with moss, limbs greening
in their rainy sleeves.

Innumerable are its fingers, bony and grey
and forever dropping to earth, pointing *where?*
when the wind says *move!*

Slowly it renders its leathery clumps
in late spring, as if
indecisive or coy,

leaves palming insects that spit their
fine contempt upon our cars
and patio furniture

or drop writhing slivers of green
voracious on summer threads
to strip the apple tree and roses.

Some years the leaves crackle
with gall, freckled and pocked
and yellowed

but the oak perseveres
sacred to the god of thunder
to whom it sacrifices its worn out limbs

in storms, shaking them mad
until brittle pulp shatters
on roadways.

As summer begins, catkins
litter our pristine lawns
snag and huddle in corners of everything.

Summer ends with a persistent hail of acorns
their dusty meat harbouring
tannins and weevils

in equal measure. Squirrels
traverse the air paths between trees
descending to cache their treasure

buried in leaves I displace with my machines,
but even so will rise next spring
a new forest, misplanted in pots and flowerbeds.

## Felled

The woodsmen have been in our park
all week, flagging trees
with too little life left.

Pink ribbons proliferate
in the leafless gulf
between winter and spring.

Came again today
with their chainsaws. Smoke
like a morning mist
embittered the air
for hours.

We were warned
about wind in these trees
how it might pull sodden roots
loose after storms. Beds of needles
freshened the paths some mornings;
branches laid themselves over mud
allowing clean passage.

Now this. Logs wallow
still netted in ropes of ivy, cut
before they were pulled to earth
and here they lie, will lie until spring
can pull some covering over them.

They were all ages, it seems. Hearts
exposed where they fell. Edges raw.
Holes gape where the birds
drilled nests in hollow trees,
honeycombed galleries of woodworm
brought down to earth.

These bright scars
on the stumps will someday
seal themselves in a shroud of bark,
the severed limbs
sink and soften, frass and fungi
becoming future ground.

# Skunk Cabbage

*Lysichiton americanus*

Spring rises from the black swamp
of this narrow scrap of park
squeezed between houses
and playing fields. Gold
and green eclipse the litter
of wind-flung branches
in brackish water, the air bruised
with skunk where some
living thing brushed its leaves
in haste for food
or escape or parenthood.

The petals of its golden spathe
cup the risen spadix
as a lantern its flame
and to its light
come the flies and rove beetles,
relishing its glow and fetor,
swarming the mounds
of its tiny flowers
in the refuge
of its hills and valleys.

## Spring Storm

Trees, barely in leaf, thrash
their argumentative limbs,
unable to speak. Later in the season
their voices will multiply: accusatives
waxing sibilant in a summer storm.

But spring is all mute fury. The beating
of empty fists on the window, wrenching
bud from branch, fistfuls of birds
seeding the wind. This season, the rain
will be all that speaks, slapping
itself on the pavement,
gashing the soil.

We have gone beyond thirst, it seems.
The skin of the earth
too old and tired to open
and accept, the clouds too angry
to be gentle. They blacken
with all they have held back.

Water runs where it will,
taking with it
all that we have planted.
It's almost a relief
the burden of all that care
swept out of reach.

The earth's crust is melting
beneath the rain, diminishing
the work of millennia
to a stain in the storm drain
that will plume and settle
its blanket of silt
to silence the ocean floor.

## Meadow at Dusk

Into this murk the salamander
slips its small majesty. A slender
entry wave settles without trace.

The brack ripples with skittering life,
winged and stick-legged, soft
and brittle. This is a broad church
whose hymns are the chirps
and clacks of the night chorus.

Every shadow holds more life
beneath its lip, each vertical
a ladder for something, every leaf
a lid or bowl or nursery.

Some flowers, having tracked the sun
all day, dip their heads to evening.

Others pour their hearts into making roots
larding their store of sunlight
into bulbs the colour of winter moons,
or send their thoughts downward
in search of rock dust or moisture.

There is that conversation they have,
dense and microbial, a barter
worked out over millennia: swapping
sweet secretions for simple nourishment.

And as the season churns belowground
folding themselves into soil.

# Part 4

"There is more wisdom in your body than
in your deepest philosophy."
—Friedrich Nietzsche

## Devil Spawn of the Devil Grass Wheat

Number one enemy of the gut,
down it comes through the entry tube
of ourselves: a thousand times a year maybe
this same trip. Spoiling for trouble.

Our gut gets tired of fighting it
this protein fraction itching to ford
the tight junctions of our mucosal lining.

It's just another thug hanging around
the epithelium, up to no good. For years
the bouncers throw it out,
kick it into the body's sewer, tell it not to come back.

But at breakfast, lunch, there it is again, same crooked grin
as it pushes past, until finally
perhaps the bouncers have had a bad night,
some irksome molecule
throwing its weight around,
wearing them down,
diverting attention.

Off in one dark corner
something changes hands,
the door cracks open, and finally
the gluten slips through.

There's more unpleasantness. The lymphocytes
move in, their memory cells
deranged and working overtime. Suddenly everyone's
a suspect, being hauled off, protests
ignored, a massive case of mistaken identity.

Riots erupt in the body's distant suburbs.
Fires burn in the gut, the turning places of the knees.
Up in the brain there's confusion: fog rolls in
even while the sun shines. Sometimes the battles flare up
overnight, waking the body from its slumbers with a sense
someone's moving around downstairs.

## Be Vigilant My Body

In every cell
attend to the signals of disorder.
Guard the synaptic cleft,
let it leap with the orderly firing.
Let it carry the messages of balance.

Be not too vigilant as I sleep,
keep me from miscommunication:
the taut nerves, the pulled muscle,
the agonizing cramp. Do not speak to me
of deferred pain, or the knots and puzzles
of age, predictable faults
in the patterns of efficiency
that homeostasis once laid down.

I have no training in mortality,
this body's gibberish, its frayed connections
and failures to respond. Who is there
to teach me the language of disharmony
but my own worn vessel, its thermostats
askew, its packaging less taut, circuits
less reliable. The fevers of midlife
have come at last
to rove about this house and
feed upon me in the night.

## Amnesia

So much to forget. Who wouldn't
want to? That pesky debt hanging
over a life that's starting to sour.
The car that won't start. The fridge
that won't freeze. The man who forgets
to come home at night.

Bang. Put the lights out,
if you will, on this life. Walk
into a new untarnished one,
not even a name to anchor you.

How to gather the self for a remake
without the hooks of memory
snagging the events
that mark us? How to lose
the scents that lock us
to a meal, a man, a moment
in a spring-drenched field?

We are in search of the never mind,
the mind that never
drags us back to old wounds,
thus healing them.

And if we can't have that
then give us sleep,
the kind we wake from as if
from long surgeries,
everything excised
but some pain, nagging
like a song with no lyrics
or a scar with no story.

# Home is a Different Country

*Now I am back*
*And home is a different country*
                              —John Burnside

The house has never been cleaner
the streets quieter
the buses more empty
churning the night, every light on,
every seat free
but one.

Life has got
so small. There is no front
to report from.
Everywhere you look you
don't see It.
No one yet knows
what It looks like
so it's hard to hide from.

Still, we take shelter
and measures against It.
Our hands have never been cleaner
our larders more curiously stocked
our agendas more empty.

TV lights flicker
in the neighbours' curtains
as if they had company
into the small hours.
The news, the news, the news.

I stay home, a new cliché.
Sewing masks.
Baking bread.

Wither now
the woman from the pool
with the evil eye.
The ill-tempered waitress
from the coffee shop.
The bastard who left me.

A cold bright spring
pours its heart out.
The mountains
have never been clearer.

On walks the strangers pass
averting faces as if
a glance might smite them.

Out shopping
we play sluggish games of hopscotch
on the floor's markings.
Everything takes longer.

Trying not to breathe
we mumble in our masks,
gesture with our raw clean hands.

Wolves and cougars
take a few liberties
in our empty streets.

The sun in children's paintings
has always been
the colour of the tape
now enfolding our playgrounds.

## Every Night I Catch My Breath

And force it down into
the dark damp places
where it speaks quietly
to my heart.

My breath whispers that I
am alive. It makes promises.
It carries the scent of lilacs
that have roused themselves
again, and overwhelmingly.

I think of flowers that open
each morning and close
at night. Every day for the
whole of their lives.

When I breathe I think
of my father's breath
that made the sound of water
straining air when he died.

Late at night, when the world
outside is quiet
my breath tries to still
the staccato of my heart.

## Colour Blind

The snow is mute on the subject
offering all or nothing to its
own blind followers while you
live in vision's winter full time,

misreading the maps of the world
robbed of their reds or greens,
your highways delimited
by walls of lush, taupe foliage.

Maybe every stop light is amber
maybe every eye blinks brown
maybe your red balloon vanished
long ago in a high summer field.

I am your interpreter
in the court of the paint-seller.
I lead you through buildings
with their helpful coloured signs

and feed you on fruits and leaves
in desert hues. You pour us wine
as dark as a twilit river, as black
as your blood runs, and mine.

## The Other Eye

One night I stepped into a darkness
that crackled with nonexistent light. Flashes
in my periphery that illuminated
nothing.
        By morning
they were gone. Then
my gaze muddied
without cause.
        One speck
spattered itself
where only I could see.

Now the stars in my other sky
drift in a snarl of threads,
meteor tails of blood and vitreous.

From here
there will be
birds in every sky, distant
and elusive.

My own private climate change.
One eye's glaciers melting
as the world ages
within.

## Solstice

A long time coming. Long days
filled with the ink of
too much daylight. Love

like a risen sun, reluctant
to set, and then does: a golden tree
stripped in a day by an autumn gale,

one day in leaf, the next
a tangle of black like the sudden nest
of veins that threatened

a curtain of dark; my vision
stabbed back into place with light;
a seasonless ache that drowns in the eye's black well

and a spray of black stars
to remember it by, in white rooms
or bright skies. And now this. October's rug

pulling the world from beneath me.
Since then, as the year trickles
to an end, I've been waiting for the balance

to shift, for light to dilute
and leak away.
Give me a darkness

to sleep through, capable night pushing light
off the margins. A life-sized darkness to cure
the ills of summer.

# Penumbra

The day of the solar eclipse the shadows
of trees split into crescent moons on the pavement
Look, I said to the dog, the world has changed

There was a chill in the air and the light went glassy
A man passed us offering UV glasses to families
laying out their solar eclipse picnics and afraid to look at the sun

I was waiting outside the café when it happened
and a man came out with a welder's mask and said
Do you want a look
and I saw the lack of it as the moon slid its face
over the face of the sun as if its colder twin

And that is when I went walking
and everywhere the sun littered the ground
falling from the trees in its thousands
as it waned and waxed
releasing us from heat and light
repeating itself as if nothing on earth mattered

# Laws of Average

Take one child and compare
with another the age of the research cohort.

Add siblings, childhood accidents, the handfuls
of mercury or mouthfuls of pesticide.

Factor in parental divorce, skin colour,
home moves, the loss of esteem
or virginity, the absence or presence
of fast-food trinkets and cereal box toys,
hospital visits and near–death experiences.

Find the square root of bruises and cuts.
Average the addictions, the uncles
or priests and attitudes to food
with household income
and bedtime rituals.

Add the packaging
from common drug store items.

Run these numbers against the rate of growth,
the number of times chosen for teams,
the presence or absence of musical
or other artistic talent.

Triangulate the child-sized casts
with surgical, vaccination or emotional scars
and congenital defects.

Take academic achievement,
career prospects and the likelihood of marriage.
Add or subtract childbirths, infectious diseases, parasites
and subclinical conditions, squared with the number
of betrayals, friends and age of parental loss; plus bonus,

pension, tax and mortgage rates, and the sum total
of car, home and personal insurance.
From gross lifetime earnings
deduct the risk of dementia or heartbreak
and the likelihood of falls, the effects of isolation
and the amount of fibre missing from the diet.

Reports should include standard deviations, degrees
of freedom, and the probability your result
occurred by chance.

# The Call

Some of us will be out when it comes,
returning home to destiny's
envelope on the mat; others
curled up with a book
about to be laid flat, spine broken.

Some of us will be ready, our lives
spare and box-shaped. Many
will not, and the shambles
of departure will stifle for a while
a life that wanted
so much more before this moment.

We have worked hard to be happy,
and happiness there is
in the singular. *Only*
is our word, and we keep it
safe beneath our pillow. We dip it
in our morning tea, smooth it flat
on a table with one empty chair,
fasten it to our suitcase
when we travel; pack no more
than one hand can carry.

For though we have been chosen
we are not qualified.
We who have tended
to our own hurts, whose hearts
are chipped like mantel china,
we know little of care.
Of all day anticipating the dangers
to a brittle child, all night
attuned to the sounds
of wandering and loss.

# Notes

**Evolution of the Tick** – The ones described are dog ticks, *Dermacentor variabilis*. They carry Rocky Mountain spotted fever. The ones that carry Lyme disease are the much smaller black-legged, or deer tick, *Ixodes scapularis*. Both exhibit host-seeking behaviour that has them position themselves on grasses, leaftops and twigs, their two pairs of forelegs extended.

**Cordyceps** – There are some 600 species of this parasitic fungus, sometimes referred to as a "zombie fungus." The one in the poem, *Cordyceps lloydii*, was described as a possible mycopesticide by Paul Stamets in his book *Mycelium Running*, as it infects carpenter ants in Costa Rica, sending them to the top of the jungle canopy where the fungus fruits and sporulates from its body.

**Culatello** is an artisanal boneless cured pork product from Northern Italy, made only from a small portion of rump meat, cured in a characteristic string wrapping and produced in the province of Parma.

**Caramelized Garlic & Squash Tart** is a recipe by Yotam Ottolenghi that appeared in his "New Vegetarian" column in *The Guardian*. A version without squash can be found in his cookbook *Plenty*.

**Hügelkultur** ('hill culture' or 'mound culture') is a traditional German/East European composting technique much beloved of Permaculture practitioners: a mound of wood debris and other compostable biomass plant materials gradually decomposes and both holds water in the soil and enriches it ready for planting.

**Skunk Cabbage** – There are in fact two versions of skunk cabbage in North America, both growing in marshy, boggy areas and both having distinctive and (to humans) unattractive aromas. Both feature a spathe (a bract, or leaf) that surrounds a spadix (a spike of small flowers). *Lysichiton americanus* is the Western variety, also known as Swamp Lantern, because of its bright yellow spathe. The spathe of the Eastern variety, *Symplocarpus foetidus* is brownish-purple and green.

**Devil Spawn of the Devil Grass Wheat** – Celiac disease, celiac sprue or gluten-sensitive enteropathy, affects around 1% of the world's population. The protein zonulin controls the permeability of the tight junctions between cells that protect the gut lining, and can allow gluten molecules to enter the bloodstream to trigger an autoimmune reaction in the genetically susceptible.

There are no rules here.
Impossible things happen and we gaze
at a parent's carapace as if we
were not the ones
whose names had slid away.

Taking charge, we lead the way
as if we knew it. Begin to grasp
how random was our childhood.
We cannot fear a past
that only one of us can see.
All those threads of anger
fallen from dwindled shoulders,
the script forgotten.

We take, too long awaited,
the offerings of sweetness and need.
But for some the weight of gratitude
will be too much
when it lifts; a burden
that was always only borrowed
will leave its shape
in our weary arms.

# About the Author

AUTHOR PHOTO BY LILLIE LOUISE MAJOR

Rhona McAdam is a poet, food writer and holistic nutritionist. Born in Duncan on Vancouver Island, she began her writing career in Edmonton, Alberta, spent a dozen years working in London, UK, and studied food in Parma, Italy. She holds three master's degrees—in Library & Information Science from the University of Alberta; Communications Planning from the University of Wolverhampton; and Food Culture & Communication from the University of Gastronomic Sciences (Slow Food's university in northern Italy)—as well as a certificate in natural nutrition from the Canadian School of Natural Nutrition.

McAdam has a long-time passion for food and ecology, has worked as a cook and educator, and held a wide range of volunteer positions in food security, including fruit tree picker, grant writer, and many years in the fields and on the board of Haliburton Community Organic Farm in Victoria. After a career in information management, she now lives in Victoria where she teaches culinary classes and Eco-Nutrition at the Canadian School of Natural Nutrition. Her poems have appeared in literary journals and anthologies in Canada, the US, Ireland and the UK since the 1980s. Her ten poetry collections include the award-winning *Hour of the Pearl*, *Old Habits* (published simultaneously in the UK and Canada), *Cartography* and *Ex-Ville*. She is also the author of *Digging the City*, an urban agriculture manifesto.

# Acknowledgements

Warmest thanks are due to editors of the following where some of the poems have previously appeared:

> *Acumen, Alimentum, CV2, CuiZine,* PoetryMagazine.com, *PRISM international, Small Farmer's Journal, Trek, Victoria Times Colonist*
> *The Earth's Kitchen* (Leaf Press, 2011)
> *Sunday Dinners* (JackPine Press, 2010)
> *Sweet Water* (Caitlin Press, 2020)
> *Worth More Standing* (Caitlin Press, 2022)
> *We Are One: Poems from the Pandemic* (Bayeux Arts, 2020)

Some poems have also appeared in poetry videos, for:

> BC Seedy Saturday (Farm Folk City Folk)
> Poets Caravan (Planet Earth Poetry)

The poem "Table" (original title "Mesa") appears with the kind permission of Juan Carlos Galeano (*Amazonie/Amazonia,* Ecrits des Forges, 2007).

My deepest gratitude to Anne Berkeley, Claire Crowther, Sue Rose and Tamar Yoseloff for keeping me sane and writing during the pandemic and beyond, and for their sage advice on so many of these poems. To all at Banff Wired, Sage Hill, St Peter's Abbey, Almàssera Vella, and Chateau Ventenac for time, inspiration and companionship during residencies and workshops over the years it has taken to assemble these poems. To David Godkin for close readings and encouragement. To Carlo Petrini, the Unisg community and Slow Food campaigners everywhere for eco-gastronomic teachings and inspiration. And to my enviro-lit buddies Gyorgyi Voros, Jennifer Wheat and Anna Ford for inspiring poems for our panel at the memorable ASLE Moscow Idaho conference.